THE GREATNESS
of the
GOSPEL

MEDITATIONS ON THE
GREATEST STORY EVER TOLD

BILL JENKINS

WESTBOW
PRESS®
A DIVISION OF THOMAS NELSON
& ZONDERVAN

WestBow Press books may be ordered through booksellers or by contacting:

WestBow Press
A Division of Thomas Nelson & Zondervan
1663 Liberty Drive
Bloomington, IN 47403
www.westbowpress.com
844-714-3454

ISBN: 978-1-6642-9900-9 (sc)
ISBN: 978-1-6642-9899-6 (e)

Library of Congress Control Number: 2023908162

Print information available on the last page.

WestBow Press rev. date: 05/10/2023

CONTENTS

INTRODUCTION

The Beginning of the Gospel
Read Mark 1:1–8

Mark began his telling of the story of Jesus with these words: "The beginning of the gospel of Jesus Christ." These words are like a starting gun at the beginning of a footrace. Mark saw the miraculous in the preaching of the gospel and began his account with a sense of wonder and expectation. Everything was fresh and new. Everything was filled with wonder. Mark set out to tell us about it with energy and enthusiasm. "The beginning of the gospel of Jesus Christ, the Son of God ..." He set a hook in the hearts of readers with these words. It is God's story—the greatest story ever told.

Mark was not at all like that fellow in Kentucky in 1809 who asked, "Any news down't the village, Ezry?"

"Well, Squire McLain's gone t' Washington t' see Madison swore in, and ol' Spellman tells me this Bonaparte fella has captured most of Spain. What's new out here, neighbor?"

"Nuttin'. Nuttin' a' tall 'cept for a new baby born t' Tom Lincolns. Nuttin' eva happens out here. I believe they's callin' em Abe."

Mark was excited about telling the story of Jesus. Someone great had been born. Something significant had happened, and he wanted to tell the world about it. Mark did not begin with the birth of Jesus as Matthew and Luke did. Still he knew that at the heart of the story he is about to tell is God's incarnation in Jesus of Nazareth.

"The beginning of the gospel of Jesus Christ, the Son of God, as it is written in the Prophets ..." Mark knows the story began way back there. History is not a random kaleidoscope of disconnected events. It is a process directed by God, who has plans and purposes to fulfill. Marcus Aurelius said it well: "The things of God are full of foresight."

Mark set out to tell a story that had never been told before about an event that had never happened before and could not possibly have happened—but it did. It is a good-news story. There has never been a generation of people not hungry for good news. It was so in Mark's day when John the Baptist came out of the wilderness with the good news that the Messiah was at the door, and all the land of Judea went out to him.

"But that's nothing," said Mark. "You should have been there when John stepped aside and Jesus took the lead. From border to border and bank to bank an excitement filled the land of promise.

"The Messiah, Jesus, the Son of God, has walked and talked among us and is with us still. I want to tell you about the sick folks who were healed and the deranged folks who were put in their right minds. I want to tell you how whole cities and towns came out to hear Him and how the entire countryside hung on His every word. I want to tell you how He forgave sinners so compassionately and inspired hope in the hopeless. I want you to know how He empowered the requirements of the law by changing people's hearts.

"I must tell you how the elements of nature bowed to His will and obeyed His every word. I must tell you how the world turned against Him and how His closest friends ran off when He was arrested.

"You've just got to hear the story of His execution and how He was left to die in the dark. And then—are you ready for this? You're going to have a hard time believing it, but I've got to tell you how He returned to life again and turned the world upside down.

"Oh, yes," said Mark, "this is a story like no other. It is a world-encompassing, soul-satisfying, never-ending, ever-growing story. I could write for a thousand years and fill a thousand libraries and never catch up to it, could never tell but … the beginning of the gospel of Jesus Christ, the Son of God."

The gospel of Jesus Christ is like the first sprig of green in a dusty heart; it is a fresh breeze across our barren hopes; it is like a gentle rain on our inflamed passions. Mark wanted us to know that Jesus is still here. He still speaks above the noise and rage of a fallen world. "Come close," said Mark, "and listen to the beginning of the gospel of Jesus Christ." The beginning of the gospel brings hope and promise wherever we are. It is by far the greatest story ever told.

In the few chapters that follow we will consider the greatness of the gospel in several of its various facets, from the greatest beginning to the greatest victory. Quite often the writer uses the word *great* to describe an event or a person; other times the greatness is inherent in them. Scripture references are offered to assist in your meditations.

ONE

THE GREAT BEGINNING

Read John 1:1–14.

There are two books of the Bible that begin with "In the beginning": the Gospel of John and Genesis. Each of these books tells of divine intervention and a beginning. Consider Genesis. "In the beginning God created …" Everywhere in this vast universe, one hundred thousand light-years beyond the most distant quasar, God was—and is—creating. He inhabits the Milky Way and the emptiness between countless swirling galaxies. His presence fills the universe beyond the reach of our most powerful telescopes. Astronomers can't observe any place where God is not present.

Yet reason tells us that at some long-forgotten point in eternity's past, there was nothing—only a lonely silence. Not a silence from the absence of noise, but a deeper, frightening silence. Not a silence of emptiness, but a blind silence of nothingness. Then God spoke. Within this vast void of silence, a faint quiver was heard. Or was it felt? The soft vibration of proton, neutron, and electron, then another, and another, and another until the eternal emptiness vibrated with the energy of existence. In an event buried deep inside the memory of the original molecule, the beginning began. As great destinies swing on small hinges, so do great beginnings have small origins. In the beginning was a word spoken by the Word, and there lies a greatness far beyond the sum total of human comprehension.

"In the beginning ..." Such a phrase is most difficult to comprehend; the greatness of it stretches our imaginations to the breaking point. We reach further and further into our consciousness until it seems we'll fall off the edge of sanity, off the universe, searching for an event older than Genesis 1:1. It must have been there: that lonely, forgotten point in eternity when there was nothing—not the twinkling of a single star to light the darkness, no planets, no suns, no solar systems, no galaxies, no universe—nothing but a lonely silence. It is precisely at this point that the writer of Genesis begins. "In the beginning God created ..."

Perhaps creation began with the quiver of a single hydrogen atom. Over eons, it gathered momentum until it sounded like a great drumroll, and then, like the clashing cymbals in an orchestra pit, the explosion of a hundred billion suns shattered that lonely silence, and God nurtured His great enterprise into existence. I can no more believe that creation is the result of blind chance than I can believe *Webster's Unabridged Dictionary* is the result of an explosion in a print shop, which would be more plausible.

There is a great mystery in Genesis 1:1. But there is a greater mystery in John 1:1, 14 (NKJV). "In the beginning was the Word and the Word was with God, and the Word was God ... And the Word became flesh and dwelt among us."

Here we have, in a few verses, the doctrine of the nature and eternal existence of Jesus Christ. He was God's coworker in the creation enterprise, the cohabitant with God in the created order. All things were made through Him, and without Him nothing would exist. Just as God is without beginning or end, so is Jesus. Just as God cannot be confined to any measurement, so it is with Jesus. In the book of Revelations, Jesus is the Alpha and the Omega, the beginning and the end, the first and the last.

Great as the beginning was when God began to create, it was not so great a beginning as when His Son became one of us. As with Genesis 1:1, in John 1:1, we are confronted with the incomprehensible: the conception by the Holy Spirit, the virgin birth, the very idea that God would get involved. E. Stanley Jones reminded us,

> Apart from Jesus we know little about God. If we try to know God by starting from God we do not start from God, but from our ideas about God, but our ideas about God are not God. We must start from *God's idea about Himself,*

and God's idea about Himself is Jesus. Jesus is God breaking through to us. He is the great simplification … God speaking to us in the only language we can understand, a human language; showing us His life in the only way we can grasp it, a human life; uncovering His character in the place where your character and mine are formed, a human character. Jesus is the human life of God. He is God become intimate.

We cannot begin to comprehend the dynamics involved on God's part or on the part of Jesus when God became like us. Consider if you will that Jesus did not possess a body before He was born in Bethlehem. Consider if you *can* the consequences of becoming human—exchanging the wonders of heaven for the desolations of earth, confinement within a body with all the demands it makes, and severing a unique relationship He had known with God from before the beginning of creation. Consider that once His birth occurred, He could *never* return to an existence without a bodily form. Consider that after His death and resurrection, His body still bore the marks of the nails and thorns. Though His body was a resurrected and glorified one, it was still a body—something He would never be free from. When God's Son became flesh and dwelt among us, He accepted thereafter an eternal bodily existence that He had not known before. For eternity, this body would bear the scars of the price of our redemption.

In the beginning God created the heavens and the earth. (Genesis 1:1 NKJV)

In the beginning was the Word and the Word was with God and the Word was God. And the Word became flesh and dwelt among us. (John 1:1 NKJV)

Was ever a beginning as great as the beginning of the gospel of Jesus Christ?

TWO

THE GREATNESS OF
THE GOSPEL

Read Matthew 11:1–15.

It was a dark time in the life of the greatest human ever to
see the light of day. A darkness deeper than his dungeon
cell crowded around him. It began when the shadow of a
doubt drifted over his soul. Having lingered about the corners
of his cell for many days, the shadow became bold enough to
perch upon his shoulder and whisper in his ear, "You've made
a mistake. He's not really the Messiah. You've made a big
mistake."

Day by day the shadow whispered, and hour by hour John
the Baptist repelled its suggestions. John's life was hanging by a
thread. The axe of the executioner was being sharpened by the
hatred of Herod's wife. He had done what he could to perform

the will of God. He had never wavered in his sense of divine purpose. Not once had he taken a step back from an evil and adulterous society.

On the day Messiah was revealed to him, the sun did shine brightly. The heavens opened, and a voice declared the consummation of his ministry. "This Jesus is my Son, whom I love; with him I am well pleased (Matthew 3:17 NIV)."

John knew that voice. It was the same voice that had kept him company in the wilderness—the same voice that had given him his marching orders. It was the voice of God, and it had called him to make a straight path for the Messiah. (It is not an easy thing to make a straight path in a crooked world.) For his efforts, John was deprived the freedom of the wilderness. Shut in by four walls, he could not feel the wind upon his cheeks or the warm sunshine upon his skin or hear clearly the voice that had kept him company in the lonely night watches under desert stars. Now all he could hear, see, and feel was the ominous shadow lurking in the silence of his cell, taunting him with unsettling thoughts.

"You've made a mistake. Jesus isn't really the One to come. You will die a failure. Messiah is a myth."

Friendly faces broke through the gloom and appeared at the opening in the dungeon door. They smiled broadly, bringing news of disciple deeds.

"Do you have a message for the Master, John? Should we see Him soon, He will surely ask about you."

John answered, "No message, just a question. Ask Him this for me, my friends. I need to know if He is the One who is to come or if I should expect someone else. Tell Him I have always believed, but it would be a great comfort to hear Him say the words plainly. It would make dying easier."

Almost as an afterthought, the resounding voice that had once shattered the silence of the wilderness said quietly, "Tell Him whatever happens, it was all worthwhile. I regret nothing." A moment later, the retreating steps of his friends disappeared in the sunshine. John was left alone in his dark dungeon cell to wrestle with the shadow and await their return.

Some days later, Jesus sent a reply to John. Knowing that actions speak where words fail, Jesus said simply, "Tell John the blind are seeing, the lame are walking, lepers are being cleansed, the deaf hear, and the dead are raised."

These are the miraculous happenings that witnessed to the unchained power of God in the world, but they were not evidence of the Messiah. Such miracles as these were common among the prophets of old. The clincher for John's faith and the silencer of the shadow was the last bit of evidence, which is given status among the greatest of all miracles: "and the Gospel is preached to the poor."

With that announcement, Jesus threw open the door of heaven and welcomed the world into the kingdom of God. The kingdom is no longer the property of the Jew, no more the possession of the privileged. The greatness of the Gospel is that "God so loved the world." It is, "Whosoever will may come." It is, "Come unto Me all." Across this land of ours and around the world a miracle happens every time someone dares to declare the Gospel of Jesus Christ. Throughout this world today millions of believers and tens of thousands of unbelievers sit under the preaching of the Gospel and never consider their experience in the same category as the lame walking, demons expelled, the blind seeing, or the dead rising. The sense of wonder has long faded, familiarity has bred boredom, over-exposure has jaded the spirit that does not see the miracle in the preaching of the Gospel.

The preaching of the Gospel is a perpetual miracle, born over the fields of Bethlehem on the night the angels announced, "Good tidings of great joy." So great has been the preaching of the Gospel that men and nations, principalities and powers have been spellbound by its message. By the law of proportion, it should have faded long ago. By the law of supply and demand, it has covered the earth. The Gospel of Jesus Christ is the single greatest commodity in all the world. There is no other treasure, no other counsel equal to it. Wherein lies the greatness of the Gospel of Jesus Christ? It is in the power it has to change lives.

No movement, whatever it may be, can be greater than the people who are associated with it. The noble virtues attributed to the men and women who have embraced the Gospel are testimony to its greatness. They have been people of great courage and faith, of strong convictions and character. They were people who made allegiance to God, to His Kingdom, and to His Son, the prime directive of their lives. People who could not be bought with pleasure, threatened with death, intimidated by power, or bribed with privilege and wealth. These were people whose sacrifices were not the tokens of giving up chocolate for the forty days of Lent, but of giving their bodies as a sacrifice for the cause of Christ.

How did the heroes of the Christian faith get to be the way they were? It began for them the way it does with us today. They paused from the routine of their lives long enough to hear the preaching of the Gospel. It entered their ears, roamed around their minds, reached down and took hold of their hearts, and by its inherent power changed their lives. It gave them a new standard of behavior. The greatest struggles of any civilization are behavioral—how to live and act, how to overcome evil with good, how to achieve that sense of "ought" which keeps pressing upon the conscience of humankind. The Gospel empowers people to live above the animal level. It enlightens them to understand what is the good and acceptable will of God. The Gospel allows no evil, tolerates no injustice, condemns all wrongs, and transcends every code of ethics.

The Gospel's greatness has been authenticated in the lives of those who have embraced it. Over and above all else, the greatness of the Gospel lies in its main character—Jesus, the Christ, the Son of God, our Savior. If it were about any other person, this Gospel would be impotent. It is the person of Jesus Christ who empowers the Gospel to win the hearts of men and women, and boys and girls. It is Jesus Himself who endows the Gospel with greatness.

For angels to announce the birth of just another prophet or just another teacher would not have merited the glorious and resounding accompaniment of the heavenly choir singing "Glory to God in the highest." The distinctiveness of the glad tidings of great joy is the pronouncement that "Unto you is born a Savior." Whether we are living under Judean skies with the watchful eye of Rome upon us or living in the land of the pilgrim's pride with the eyes of Texas upon us, we need a Savior! It is not enough that the Gospel would tell about the life and teachings of Jesus. It is not enough that it should contain a grand and noble ethic. It is not enough that the Gospel should survive twenty centuries and become the most read story in the history of world. This is not enough. Unless this Gospel were great enough to transform our lives and deliver us from despair, it is of no use to us at all. It would be just another enthusiastic tale. A Gospel that leaves us struggling in our sins and uncertain in our salvation is not good news. The Gospel that makes a difference must possess a power to deliver us from the law of sin and death. The law shows us our sins; the Gospel shows us our Savior. The law shows us our condemnation; the Gospel shows us our redemption. The law says, "You are a sinner!" The Gospel says, "Your sins are forgiven!" The law says, "Pay the debt!" The Gospel says, "Jesus paid it all!"

When John's disciples reported to him that among the miracles Jesus was performing was the preaching of the Gospel, the shadow of doubt was dispelled, and a bright light broke upon his soul. Before long Salome would dance to the pleasure of Herod and bend to the will of her wicked mother. The executioner would call on John the Baptist, with an axe in one hand and a silver platter in the other; but all is well with the great prophet. He had kept the faith. He had prepared the way.

Messiah had come. The Gospel had been preached, and the devil didn't stand a chance.

Is the Gospel Out-of-Date?

Is the mind of modern man so developed that
he can
Set aside the Gospel news, as beneath his lofty
views?
Has the Gospel proved of late to be something
out-of-date?
Something that has fell behind all the progress
of mankind?
True, the Gospel's been around quite a spell, so
has the ground.
Who but fools would dare to state mother earth
is out-of-date?
Soil still gives its strength to seeds, meeting all
each body needs;
Yet, all the soil in man's control cannot feed a
hungry soul.
Gospel truths alone can give strength by which
the soul must live.
This "Good News" can never be out-of-date,
for you and me!

—Arthur Slater

THREE

THE GREATEST GOOD NEWS

Read: Luke 2:1–14.

On Christmas Eve 1944, a small group of ragged men huddled together behind the barbed wire and brick walls of the Nazi prison camp Dachau. They had gathered to worship. The preacher for the evening was Martin Neimoller. Before coming to Dachau, Niemoller had spent three years in solitary confinement as Hitler's personal prisoner at Sachsenhausen. As one who resisted Hitler, he had been charged with treason. As he stood before the eager listeners in Dachau, he took inspiration from Luke 2:10 (NKJV): "Do not be afraid, for behold I bring you good tidings of great joy which shall be to all people."

He began: "When Christmas must be celebrated in captivity, it is naturally a rather dismal affair. Under such circumstances there remains little chance for the joy of the heart as we knew it formerly in the Christmas days … We are now a people who walk in darkness; men who are tossed back and forth between fear and hope and who finally find nothing better to do than to let things take their course."

In that dismal and hopeless situation, Martin Niemoller went on to preach the glory of Christmas and the grandeur of Christ, saying, "Christ, the God with us, is also the God for us. And we, dear friends, who are cut off from the outside world, inactive spectators of all men's battles and convulsions, should not the saying about 'good tidings of great joy concern us in particular, since we know fear- fear of death as well as fear of life? Let us therefore today, implore the Lord Jesus Christ that He may enter also into us, bring us His salvation, and grant us His great joy" (20 Centuries of Great Preaching, X, pp. 241–246).

How is it possible that an age-old message of good news could be relevant to prisoners marked for extinction? It is because this is not your ordinary good news. On a hillside in Judea the startling announcement was made by ambassadors from the court of heaven: "Do not be afraid, for behold, I bring you good tidings of great joy which will be to all people. For there is born to you this day in the city of David a Savior, who is Christ the Lord" (Luke 2:10, 11 NKJV).

Over the armed camp of that hard old Roman world the song of the angels rang out, like the bells of the city of God. A crescendo of heavenly music rolled from the far corner of the universe and flooded the shepherd's field: "Glory to God in the highest, And on earth peace, goodwill toward men" (Luke 2:10, 11 NKJV).

This is not the peace and goodwill we have for one another, for we know that is something not yet realized. This is the peace and goodwill God has toward us. That, my friends, is good news— the world's *greatest* good news! God is not mad at us. God loves us, and Christmas is the evidence of His love. No other news was ever announced quite like this. At long last one greater than any other arrived upon our shores. He had been a long time promised.

Countless eyes closed in faith before the Savior came. Many weary backs bent with age in Herod's day, clinging to the hope God would act. Many hearts almost failed for fear that God had forgotten His promises of old. There was old Simeon, who had waited long years for the consolation of Israel. There was Anna, a prophetess smitten with old age, looking for the redemption of Israel (Luke 2: 25–38). Whether under the heel of Caesar or Hitler or terrorists, Christmas speaks across the years to quiet doubt, remove despair, and vanquish fear. God rules the world. He does not forget His promises, and in the fullness of time He brings them all to pass, confounding our expectations.

We have our share of news today, and most of it is bad. When people discuss the condition of our world today, we hear it said often: "Why doesn't God do something?" *Why doesn't God do something?* Have we become so calloused to the magnitude of the message sung by the multitude of heavenly hosts? My good friends, God has done something! Unto us is born a Savior! Turn over a few pages to Luke 4, and we discover what this means to us. Beginning with verse 17, it means: the preaching of good news, the healing of broken hearts, the deliverance of the captive, the granting of vision to the blind, freedom for those who are caught in the swelling unrest of life, the declaration of the year of acceptance, and the day of salvation.

It is precisely now when God lays the question at our doorstep and asks, "Why don't you do something about what I have already done? Believe the Gospel and live."

Christmas means two things. It first means we needed a Savior. The prophet Isaiah described the world before Christ as "the land of the shadow of death" and the inhabitants as "people who walked in darkness" (Isaiah 9:2 NKJV). Our Christmas hymns harken back to that time.

> In the bleak mid-winter, frosty wind made moan;
> Earth stood hard as iron, water like a stone;
> Snow had fallen, snow on snow,
> In the bleak mid-winter, long ago. (Christina Rossetti)

> Come thou long expected Jesus, born to set Thy people free
> From our fears and sins release us, let us find our rest in Thee. (Charles Wesley)

What this world needed was someone to lead it out of darkness, away from death and decay— someone to break the power of Satan's hold upon the hearts and wills of humankind. We needed a Savior.

The second thing Christmas tells us is that God gave the world what it needed at the right time: a Savior "who comes to break oppression, to set the captive free, to take away transgression and rule in equity" (James Montgomery).

Some may say the world is still a place of darkness with wars and crime and fear and lawlessness. Sadly, that is true, but there is now one definite advantage. There is a light shining in the darkness, and all who will may follow it. You see, before Christ the world could not help being what it was. Now it has a choice. Christmas tells us that the world does not have to be the way it is today. Peace can prevail and righteousness and mercy can flow down like a mighty waterfall if only we would do something about what God has already done.

Suppose I was about to die of a terrible disease for which there was no cure. Then suppose a cure was discovered and offered to me. Before, I did not have a choice, but now I do. I can live or die. The choice is no longer left to blind chance, but to me. If I were to refuse the medicine, its ability to make me whole again would not be diminished at all, but my ability to live and be whole would be. What if I were dirt poor and lived in terrible circumstances and someone offered me great wealth? Before, I did not have a choice, but now I do. I can continue in my poverty, or I can escape it. The choice is mine. If I should refuse the wealth, its value would not be reduced one penny; however, my poverty would be considerably greater because I had refused the opportunity to be other than I was. It is always good news to have a choice between what you are and what you could become.

There is a light shining in the darkness—the light of the life of Jesus Christ, our Savior. The greatest good news is that no matter who we are, no matter what we are, no matter where we are, no matter what we have done or left undone, we have a Savior, which is Christ the Lord: Son of Mary, Son of man, Son of God. This Savior loves us, cares about us, and readily forgives our sins. This Savior heals us, strengthens us, and gladly cleanses our hearts. This Savior was born for us, lived for us, died for us, and rose from death for us. There has never been any greater news than this. Our world needs these good tidings of great joy.

> For our world today, with all its turmoil and tragedy,
> Christmas is the eloquent reminder that God
> has not given up on humanity. (Frank Gaeblein)

God is still doing today what He did in Bethlehem on that first Christmas:

> He's leading wise men to worship, sending angels down to sing,
> Pointing shepherds to a stable to behold their God and King.
> He's lighting candles in the darkness, bringing peace upon the earth.
> It is the time for earth's redemption; it is the night of Jesus's birth.

This is the greatest good news.

FOUR

THE GREATEST PERSON

Read Matthew 12:1–8, 38–42.

I n these verses from the Gospel of Matthew we discover the greatest person ever to be born. His name is Jesus of Nazareth, the Son of Mary, a.k.a., the Christ. Norman Vincent Peale wrote of Jesus:

> Standing solitary and alone, like some majestic Everest or Gibraltar,
> Jesus Christ towers over the landscape of human history.
> There never was anyone like Him, before or since.
> By His greatness He has reshaped the destiny of mankind and
> Divides our time as before and after Him.

He is the sensation of the ages.

An Athenian philosopher once said of Him,

"The Galilean is too great for our small hearts."

More than any other person ever born, Jesus was born for greatness. The angel said to Mary, "And behold, you will conceive in your womb and bring forth a Son, and shall call His name Jesus. He will be great." (Luke 1:31, 32 NKJV).

Surely our souls have not become so insensitive that we can pass through the Christmas celebration and escape without feeling a tingle of excitement at the greatness of it all: the virgin birth; the visitations of Gabriel, who stands in the presence of God; the serenade of angels on a hillside in Judea; the worship of wise men from the east; the nativity star that led their way. This is not the common and ordinary we are dealing with. This is nothing less than the world's greatest birthday party for the greatest person ever born.

Jesus grew up in the shadows of Israel's heroes. Moses, Abraham, Jacob, David, and a host of others occupied the Jewish hall of fame. At some time in His life a certain awareness came to Him of His own preeminence. In John's Gospel Jesus is compared to the heroes of Israel.

A Samaritan woman asked Jesus, "Are you greater than our father Jacob, the well-digger?"

Jesus replied, "Yes, I am."

The Jews asked, "Are you greater than our father Abraham?"

Jesus replied, "Abraham rejoiced to see my day; before Abraham was born, I AM. Yes, I am greater than Abraham."

The Jews considered that David had been their greatest king. Jesus reminded them that their great king had referred to the Christ as "my Lord."

John the Baptist was a local hero in Jesus's day; but John said of Jesus, "He must increase, but I must decrease."

A measure of the greatness of Jesus is revealed when He was challenged for His apparent disregard of the holy Sabbath. To those who accused Him, Jesus answered, "I am the Lord of the Sabbath."

The angel said to Mary, "Call your Son Jesus; for He will be great."

How great is He? The Temple was the center of the nation of Israel, the most sacred spot on earth, the "house of God" and the "gate of heaven." Whenever Jews knelt to pray anywhere in the world, they knelt facing Jerusalem and the Temple mount.

In Jesus's day, Herod ordered the reconstruction of the Temple, and the task took forty-six years. Its beauty and magnificence held visitors spellbound. Built of polished white marble, its eastern front reflected the rays of the rising sun like plates of pure gold. It was a shame that the sun should ever set on such a magnificent structure.

The Jews esteemed nothing more than the Temple, except the God worshipped there. When Jesus said, "In this place is One greater than the Temple" (Matthew 12:6 NKJV), He was laying claim to deity. Who can be greater than the Temple except the One who dwells within the Holy of Holies? There He was, within an arms-reach of them, and they did not know it. The mute marble stones recognized Him and strained to praise the One for whom they existed.

The angel said to Mary, "Call your son Jesus; He will be great." How great is He? The story of Solomon and the Queen of the South is found in 1 Kings 10. The Queen of Sheba (Ethiopia) came from a long journey to test the wisdom of Solomon. She discovered Solomon was twice as wise and great as the reports she had heard.

She declared, "Blessed be the Lord your God, who delighted in you, setting you on the throne of Israel" (1 Kings 10:9 NKJV).

Solomon gave her all she desired and more so that she returned home satisfied she could discover no one greater than he. As the wisest and wealthiest man in the world, Solomon had the power and the means to satisfy the temporal desires of everyone who came to him.

But then someone came along who was greater than Solomon. Solomon's wisdom was borrowed from Him in whom is hid all the treasures of wisdom and knowledge (Colossians 2:3), borrowed from the wisdom that was operative when the world began. Solomon had nothing that was not given to him by this Greater One.

Jesus is greater than Solomon at satisfying the hungers of the heart, mind, and soul. Solomon could answer questions, but Jesus answers *needs*. Solomon could give possessions. Jesus gives peace and life. Solomon could impress you. Jesus can save you. He has never sent anyone away empty but is delighted to heap upon every searching soul His vast treasures of love, mercy, and grace—the stuff of which eternal kingdoms are made. Search out this carpenter from Nazareth, and He will give you the desires of your heart and much more.

The angel said to Mary, "Call your son Jesus, for He will be great." How great is He? The Jews wanted a sign. Jesus reminded them of Jonah, who had served as a sign to the people of Nineveh.

When Jonah stood on the capitol steps of Nineveh and delivered his message from God, he told of how he had resisted his mission. He told of how God had sent a storm after him and brought him to his destination through the bowels of a fish for the singular purpose of preaching repentance to the Ninevites. Wonder of wonders, they believed Jonah's message that God was displeased with them, repented of their wickedness in sackcloth and ashes, and received mercy from a forgiving God. But behold, someone greater than Jonah arrived on the steps of the world. He stands on street corners and in pulpits all over the world with a message from the God of heaven and earth.

Mark condenses His message this way: "Now after John was put in prison, Jesus came to Galilee, preaching the gospel of the kingdom of God, and saying, 'The time is fulfilled, and the kingdom of God is at hand. Repent and believe in the Gospel" (Mark 1:14, 15 NKJV).

Both the messenger and the message are greater than Jonah. Jonah was a sinful, rebellious man, resisting the will of God. This Greater One is sinless and embraces the will of God. Jonah sat in the shade and pouted when God spared Nineveh, preferring they be destroyed. This Greater One wept over the world, and on a hot afternoon stretched Himself upon a cross, praying for the forgiveness of His executioners. Jonah was a prophet, a spokesman for God, the middleman. This Greater One is the Son of God, the Main Man from the heart of God. The people of Nineveh acknowledged the sign of Jonah, respected his message as the sure word of God, repented, and were spared.

Jesus says the people of Nineveh will rise up in judgment on this generation and condemn it, saying, "You had a greater one than Jonah. You had a greater sign in the resurrection of Christ. You had a greater message of love and redemption. You had a greater opportunity to repent. Yet you ignored it. You brushed it aside; you counted it as mere gibberish. Therefore you, who are the generation of the Messiah, will have the greater condemnation."

The angel said to Mary, "Call your son Jesus, for He will be great." How great is He? In Hebrews 3:1–6 we are told again that He is greater than Moses. Someone greater than the Temple, greater than Solomon or Jonah or Moses or Abraham has come, requesting an audience with you. You had thought that so great a One as this would surely be unapproachable. Not so! Part of His greatness is that He is approachable.

In a sermon entitled "The Blind Man's Earnest Cry," Charles Haden Spurgeon reconstructed the conversation between blind Bartimaeus and the crowd the day Jesus came to town.

Bartimaeus cried out for the Master.

The crowd answered him, "How dare you, a beggar, interrupt such a person as Jesus, the Christ! Why, even now

He is on His way to Jerusalem to ride in triumph as the king of Israel. What can *you* be at, thinking that you, in your rags and cursed darkness, are to have an audience with such a great one as He?"

"Great One, is He!" exclaimed Bartimaeus. "Great One! I need a great one! A little one will not serve my need. It must be a great one to open my eyes; and the greater He is, the more reason I should cry out to Him."

Indeed, a Great One is what we need—one greater than our sin and separation, our loneliness and despair, our fears and failures, our hurts and sorrows. We need one great enough to deliver us from our bondages. A little one will not meet our needs.

The angel said to Mary, "God is giving you a Great One." What is your need today? Set it before your mind. Is there a hurt that needs healing, a fear that haunts you, a burden that has become unbearable, a sin that needs forgiving, a brokenness that needs mending? You need a Great One for the need you have; a little one will not do. In the closet of your heart, whisper His name, *Jesus*. Let His name echo throughout your soul, *Jesus, Jesus*. Now notice how this Great One comes to you.

FIVE

THE GREATEST MESSAGE

Read John 3:14–21.

> For God so loved the world that He gave His
> only begotten Son, that whoever believes in
> Him should not perish but have everlasting life.
> —John 3:16 (NKJV)

It's common for people who live near churches to stop
noticing the bells ringing after a while. Something similar
may be true of the ringing of the message of John 3:16.
It is one of the first Bible verses many of us learn as children.
It grows up with us, and like a ring on our finger, we become
unconscious of its presence. It is not chance that has given this
verse its unique place in the mind and heart of Christendom.
The deepest thinker sees in this verse a summation of the
Gospel message. The humblest believer feels that it expresses

simply the whole substance of his or her faith. The inspired writer gathers himself up and presents in one sweeping, comprehensive statement the majestic essence of Christian belief. After more than two thousand years the declaration still stands. In all its simple grandeur, in all its boundless love, in all its mighty power, it still stands. Centuries have passed over it and left no imprint. Time has failed to diminish its freshness. It is the same today as it was yesterday and will be forever. John 3:16 is the sum and substance of the Christian faith.

Karl Barth, the foremost theologian of the twentieth century, once spoke to a group of seminarians in Chicago, and he opened the session for questions after his address. One student asked Mr. Barth to summarize the greatest scriptural truth he had discovered throughout his illustrious career. Mr. Barth paused for a while as his audience eagerly awaited his scholarly reply. The theologian looked at his audience and replied, "It is this: Jesus loves me, this I know, for the Bible tells me so." Can there be any greater discovery from the pages of God's Holy Word than this?

If we could borrow Jacob's ladder and climb up into heaven and ask the angel Gabriel, who stands in the presence of God, to tell us of the greatest treasure heaven has to offer mankind, all he could say would be, "God so loved the world He gave His only Son in order that everyone who will believe in Him should not perish but have eternal life." This stands alone as the greatest message ever delivered to mortals. Here we have a transcending message, written not with pen and ink, but with the finger of God, spoken not by human lips, but issuing forth from the heart of God, a message shining into our world like the sun bursting through an overcast sky.

This message reveals two things about God. The first revelation is that *God loves.* The greatest theological quest of humankind has not been to discover the existence of God, but rather to discover what kind of God it is that does exist. His existence we have always believed or assumed. Our doubts have been more to what He is like. A god who does not care does not count. If he is not interested in us, how are we to be interested in him? An unknown poet put it this way: "A loving worm within the sod were better far than a loveless god." Here we are assured that God loves. Humans have hoped it. We have feared it could not be so. We have dimly dreamed and strongly doubted. We have had gods cruel, gods lustful, gods capricious, gods good-natured, gods indifferent and apathetic, but a loving God is the revelation of the Gospel of Jesus Christ. Never in all the quest of humanity do we discover a god who loves, until we encounter the One in the Holy Bible.

The second revelation about God is that *He gives.* This is always and everywhere the sign and token of love, the desire to give. The message of John 3:16 is that Someone gave and wasn't asked. A story is told by Martin Luther, the reformer, that when his translation of the Bible was being printed in Germany, pieces of the printed work fell carelessly upon the floor of the shop. One day the printer's little daughter came in and picked up a piece of paper on which the printers work had fallen. She read these words: "God so loved the world that He gave ..." The rest of the sentence was missing. It was a revelation to her.

Up to that time she had always been taught that God was to be dreaded and could be approached only through a penance. This new light upon God's nature seemed to flood her whole being with its radiance, so that her mother asked her the reason for her joyfulness. Putting her hand in her pocket, Luther tells us, the little girl handed her mother the crumbled piece of paper with the unfinished sentence. Her mother read it and asked, "He gave, did he? What was it He gave?" For only a moment the child was puzzled; she hadn't thought to ask herself that question. With the quick wisdom of a child she replied, "I don't know, but if He loved us well enough to give us anything, we need not be afraid of Him" (Hastings, Great Texts of the Bible, John, pg. 201).

God owed us nothing, yet He gave us everything. In giving us Jesus, God made a real sacrifice and impoverished Himself in the giving. If God had not truly loved us, if He had loved us only in a measure, would He not have given us only a token of His love? The love of God is such that He does not stop short of the largest possible expression of it. He gave us the most that He had to give—His beloved Son. Again, humankind's toughest struggles have not been whether or not God exists, but rather what the nature is of this God who does exist. God so loved ... God is love ... God gave. This is the greatest message given to planet earth.

> Let us continue with the verse: " ... that whosoever believes in Him should not perish, but have everlasting life."

This greatest of messages confirms what we have all–along suspected: that in this business of living we have a destiny of one sort or another. The second half of the verse can be as discomforting to us as the first half is comforting. In these words, the curtain is raised where it had always before fallen, and we are given a suggestion of what awaits us beyond this life. We are given an awareness of the awful possibility of perishing. Much of the teaching and preaching of this generation has conditioned people to too much comfort and sentimentality so that they have failed to face the prospect of perishing. Much of the greatness of this verse is due to this statement of warning. It is saying to us that at the end of the road of unbelief, the bridge is out. What compounds the tragedy of perishing is that within easy reach of everyone is the means of avoiding it. How often, after some accident or misfortune do we hear the words, "If only …, If only this … If only that …" In the end the fine line between belief and non–belief will separate the perishing with the words "If only … ; If only I had believed." This is a friendly verse of scripture, for it gives us ample warning.

The verse does not end on a note of perishing. It ends on the grand promise of a marvelous alternative: "but have everlasting life!" The end God has in view, through loving and giving, is our largest opportunity. He calls it *eternal life*. This is not mere immortality; it is much more than that. It is the fullness of everything that makes life worthwhile and existence sweet. Eternal life is more than quantity; it is quality. Eternal life is realized whenever, through Christ, a person comes to their better self and comes into a vital relationship with the ever-living, ever-loving, ever-giving God.

One cold, dark night in the city of Chicago, a blizzard was setting in.

A little boy was selling newspapers on a corner. People were in and out of the warm buildings. The little boy was so cold that he wasn't trying very hard to sell papers. He walked up to a policeman and said, "Mister, you wouldn't know where a poor boy could find a warm place to sleep tonight, would you? You see, I sleep in a box up around the corner there and down the alley, and it's awful cold in there tonight. Sure would be nice to have a warm place to stay."

The policeman looked down at the little boy and said, "You go down the street to that big white house and knock on the door. When they come to the door you just say, "John 3:16," and they will let you in."

So he did. He walked up the steps and knocked on the door, and a lady answered. He looked up and said, "John 3:16."

The lady said, "Come on in, son."

She took him in and sat him down in a rocking chair in front of a great big old fireplace. Then she left the room.

The boy sat there for a while and thought, *John 3:16 ... I don't understand it, but it sure makes a cold boy warm.*

Later the lady came back and asked him, "Are you hungry?"

He said, "Well, just a little. I haven't eaten much in a couple of days, and I guess I could stand a little bit of food."

The lady took him into the kitchen and sat him down to a table full of wonderful food. He ate and ate until he could eat no more. Then he thought, *John 3:16 … I sure don't understand it, but it sure makes a hungry boy full.*

The lady returned and took him upstairs to a bathroom where a huge bathtub was filled with warm water. He climbed into the tub and sat there soaking for a while. As he soaked, he thought, *I've not had a bath in my whole life. The only bath I ever had was when I stood in front of that big ol' fire hydrant when they flushed it out. John 3:16 … I don't understand it one bit, but it sure does make a dirty boy clean.*

The lady came and took him into a bedroom. She tucked him into a big feather bed, pulled the covers up around his neck, kissed him good night, and turned out the lights. As he lay in the darkness and looked out the window at the snow coming down on that cold night, he thought of his box in the alley. A tear trickled down his cheek as he thought, *John 3:16 … I don't understand it, but it sure gives a tired boy a soft pillow.*

The next morning the lady came up and took the boy down again to that same table full of food. After he ate, she took him to that same big rocking chair in front of the fireplace and picked up a big ol' Bible. She sat down in front of him and looked into his young face.

"Do you understand John 3:16?" she asked gently.

He replied, "No, ma'am, I don't. The first time I ever heard it was last night when the policeman told me to say it at your door."

She opened her Bible to John 3:16 and began to explain to him about Jesus. Right there, in front of that big ol' fireplace, he prayed and gave his life to Jesus.

As he watched the flames dance in the fireplace he thought, *John 3:16 … I still don't understand it, but it sure makes a lost boy feel found.*

John 3:16 is the greatest message ever given to planet Earth. I commend to you today our ever-living, ever-loving, ever-giving heavenly Father.

SIX

THE GREATEST INVITATION

Read Matthew 11:28–30.

Knowing your audience is one of the first rules of public speaking. Those Jesus spoke to that day in Galilee were, of all people, the laboring and heavy-laden. They were an oppressed people. The Lake District in Israel is rich in natural resources. The fields grow in great variety and abundance. The lake with its fish was a veritable mine of wealth. But the land was overrun by the conqueror. The farmers and the fishermen labored long and hard. Their rich crops fell before their sickles. Their nets were often full to the point of breaking. Their products sold well in the marketplace, but the tax collector stood over the threshing floor, at the boat docks, and in the marketplace and swept the profits into the emperor's hands. The wealth of Galilee went to supply the luxury of Rome. The words of the prophet Daniel were as fulfilled as ever they could be: "There shall arise in his place one who will impose taxes on the glorious kingdom" (11:20 NKJV).

Perhaps it was with a twinge of guilt or a smile of satisfaction that Matthew, the once-upon-a-time tax collector, penned these words of Christ. He is the only Gospel writer to record them. Picture that weary crowd of men and women on their way home after a hard day, stopping to listen to the young prophet. Their hands were hard, calloused, and rough. Their rugged faces were weather-tanned and smudged with daily grime. Their backs were bent, sore, and aching, and their limbs were weary from toil. They were trapped in the yoke of almost forced labor and saw no hope for rest and no cause to believe in. As they passed His way, Jesus issued the greatest of all invitations to them: "Come unto Me."

It is not often that any of us will receive invitations of prominence. While in London one summer, my wife, our daughters, and I were invited to Buckingham Palace. (Of course, we were required to produce a ticket at the door. The queen was not home at the time.) Few of us will ever dine with royalty. But if we were given the chance, we would scrub ourselves clean and wear our finest clothes. Remarkably, it has happened that the Lord of glory has stepped across the threshold of heaven, and he invites a weary world to be His guests with outstretched hands. "Come unto Me, and I will refresh you."

Whenever we consider the source of the invitation, we realize that never in the history of the world has there been a greater invitation.

It has come to us, not in gold engravings on finest parchment, but from the lips of God's own Son. It is the deity of our Lord that makes these words of His so splendid and inspiring. There is no hesitation in their tone, no apologetic note, no long argument to advance or prove His claim. It is the simple, authentic, and personal invitation of Jesus to the people of His generation and ours. (Hastings, Great Texts of the Bible, Matthew, pg. 259)

When Jesus says, "Come unto me all you who labor and are heavy laden," He is speaking to people the world over. Every life has some serious burdens, and most people have been overworked at one time or another. We have tasks to perform, responsibilities to bear, problems to solve, promises to keep, pressures that bear down upon us. Millions on the earth are bound so firmly to the economic wheel, with children to support, debts to pay, living costs to meet, that they have no prospect of freedom as long as they live. The universality of human suffering and need is one reason for the attractiveness of these words of Jesus. They strike a responsive note because much of life is a series of heavy burdens. (Elton Trueblood, "The Yoke of Christ," pg. 12)

We are a restless people, searching for straws of purpose and meaning. We are an overly emotional people, turned on by music, drugs, alcohol, entertainment, and passion. We are a transient people, moving from place to place, seeking someplace where we will be satisfied with life and living. The invitation of Christ is one of homecoming: "Come unto me. Come back home, and you will find rest for you soul." Rest for our souls! That is what we all want—the end of all our wishes and pursuits. Give us hope for this, and we will take the wings of the morning and fly to the ends of the earth to find rest for our souls. We seek for it in titles, in riches, and in pleasures. We climb up after it by ambition, come down again, and stoop for it through greed. It is not until after many miserable experiments that we are convinced of the remedy spoken by Saint Augustine fifteen centuries ago, "Our souls are restless until they rest in Thee."

The journey of a restless generation begins at the point where they wander away from God. To every generation Jesus prescribes the prerequisite for soul rest: "Learn from Me." Is it a wonder that our souls are restless? We have abandoned learning from Jesus. We have banned the Bible from our curriculum and are graduating scholars ignorant of the world's best-selling book. We argue that the words of Jesus are too old for our modern lives, that His teachings simply do not apply. This is nothing new. Five hundred years before Christ they were abandoning the law of God. The prophet Jeremiah urged the people of his generation: "Stand at the crossroads and look; ask for the ancient paths, where the good way is, walk in it, and you will find rest for your souls" (Jeremiah 6:16 NIV).

The rest Jesus offers us is not a rest divorced from labors, but a rest *within* our labors. Our soul's rest may be compared to a ship among a fleet set upon by a hurricane. While all around, the other ships are terribly shattered by the violent winds, our own ship is unaffected by the storm, being in what mariners call the eye of the storm. While the world may be coming apart at the seams, the soul that has found its rest in Jesus is a survivor. So it is with all who have the peace of God in their hearts. Thomas a' Kempis said, "A devout man carries around with him his own Comforter, Jesus, the Christ."

Even though the invitation of Jesus is universal—*Come unto Me all*—there is a singularity about it, a personal appeal. It is as though you could insert your own name in the words. "Come unto Me, Jane and John Doe, and I will give *you* rest." In the courts of law, if a person is called as a witness, no sooner is their name called than they begin to make their way to the witness box. Nobody asks, "Why is this person going there?" Or if they should say, "Who are you?" it would be enough to answer, "My name was called."

"But you are not rich. You have no golden rings upon your fingers!"

"No, but that is not the reason I go. I was called."

"You are not a person of reputation, rank, or character!"

"It does not matter. I was called."

"But you have nothing to commend you to the court."

"I only know He called my name."

So make way, doubts and fears. Make way, all sin and temptations. Make way, you hindrances of hell. Christ has called my name! You can come because Christ has called you by name. Though you have nothing to commend you before the bar of heaven, it is sufficient that Jesus has invited you (Richard Foster, Illustrations, no. 9973).

> I hear the voice call that bids me come,
> Me, even me, with all my grief oppressed,
> With sins that burden my unquiet breast,
> And in my heart the longing that is dumb,
> Yet beats forever like a muffled drum ...
>
> He bids me come and lay my sorrows down,
> And have my sins washed white by His dear grace.
> He smiles–what matters then, though all men frown.
> Nothing can assail me, held in His embrace;
> And if His welcome home the end may crown,
> Shall I not hasten to that heavenly place?
> (Hastings, Great Texts of the Bible, Matthew, pg. 266)

Since Christ has called everyone in general—and you in particular—to come and receive His peaceful rest, you know you can have it. It cannot be gotten with gold; it cannot be lost through poverty. The world cannot give it, and the world cannot take it away. It is not given on the basis of personal merit or outward circumstances. It is given only on the basis of Christ's love and your need. To that person who is not a Christian and is weary of life because of their absence from God, Christ says, "Come unto me." To that person who is a

Christian but has allowed temptations and the cares of life to overburden them, who has lost the joy of their salvation, to them Christ says, "Come unto Me, and I will refresh you." Those in their narrow corners of life with their heavy burdens, their fiery trials and temptations, their sorrows and cares, with the soil of sin upon them, Jesus calls, "Come unto Me."

Were we to have received this greatest of invitations in the form of a letter it would have read the same, "Come unto Me, all you who labor and are heavy laden, and I will give you rest." But at the bottom of the invitation would be these letters: RSVP, *repondez s'il vous plait*, Will you please respond?

SEVEN

THE GREATEST BARGAIN

Read Matthew 13:44–46.

ave I got a deal for you! Everyone likes a good bargain. Some like it so much they become easy prey to swindlers. What's the best bargain you ever got? I have been fortunate enough to have found a bargain or two in my lifetime.

In August of 1974, my wife and I were in Rome, Italy, boarding the bus for departure to the States. I had not found a suitable souvenir until I exited the hotel and met a street vendor selling small replica statues of art. I decided on one that depicted Michelangelo's Moses, but the seller quoted me a price I thought too high. I countered, and he came down a little—but not enough. I made another offer that he countered. I decided he must think I was desperate enough to pay his price, so I got on the bus and took my seat. Realizing he was going to miss his sale, he came to the window of the bus and accepted my last offer. I got back off the bus, paid him my price, and brought my treasure home. It was a bargain to me and has been in my office ever since. The vendor most likely went away thinking, *Foolish American doesn't know he was taken.*

We usually think of a bargain as something of great value gotten for a small investment. Consider that some things may be a bargain at any price. Jesus spoke of bargains in the parables of the kingdom, recorded in Matthew 13. Jesus says the kingdom of God is like a man planting a field. It is like a mustard seed, like yeast in a lump of dough, like a fishing net. There is an Oriental story about a tent made of material so delicate it could be folded to fit in the palm of one's hand. Whenever the same tent was unfolded, it provided shelter for an army of thousands. It is that way with the kingdom of God. It seems to expand and contract. Sometimes it takes the world into its embrace. Sometimes it fits easily into our hearts.

Consider two parables that appear in Matthew 13:44–46. I call these the parables of the greatest bargain in the world. Two men—a blue-collar field hand and a white-collar merchant—found something that was for them the bargain of a lifetime, worth any price to possess, and they snatched it up. Jesus is appealing to one of the most-discussed questions in the ancient world: *What is the highest good?* Answers to this question are just as eagerly sought in our modern world. What we understand to be the highest good in life reveals our personal philosophies and determines our destinies.

The question may come to us in this form: "What is there

that, if gained, will make my life worthwhile, and if lost, will make my life a failure?"

The field hand and the merchant were answering that question.

"It is the treasure in the field," said the field hand.
"It is the finest of all pearls," said the merchant.
"It is the kingdom of God," says Jesus.

In the parable of the treasure in the field we understand that the discovery was accidental. This man was digging a trench or spading the ground, and his shovel hit something hard— perhaps a large clay pot filled with gold coins just below the surface. Maybe he turned over a large rock covering a treasure chest. It appears to have been a purely accidental discovery. What he saw lit up his eyes and set his heart racing. His mind began to work out a plan whereby he could own the field and possess the treasure. He goes to the owner, who quotes him a price. The price is too high. But if he sold his house and all his possessions and took out a loan at the bank with the land as collateral, he could come up with the money. And that is exactly what he did after he made sure the deed gave him the mineral rights.

Unlike the field hand who stumbled onto his treasure by accident, the merchant had been diligently searching for quite some time for the most exquisite jewels. He had traveled through many lands and spent long hours going over displays of pearls from every culture, comparing one with another until— *eureka*! There it was! The most beautiful pearl in the world.

"How much are you asking?" he inquired.

"Sir," said the shopkeeper, "If you must ask, you cannot afford it. That is a most expensive jewel. It is priceless."

"Do not underestimate me," said the merchant. "I am a very wealthy man, and I am just as determined as I am wealthy. Name your price."

The shopkeeper sheepishly quoted a king's ransom.

The merchant didn't haggle over the price. He left the shop, cashed in his investments, and sold his other properties and possessions. He returned to the shopkeeper, owning nothing but the clothes on his back. He presented a cashier's check for the agreed price and walked away with the pearl. It now belonged to him, and he considered it to have been a bargain at any price.

Jesus said it is that way with the kingdom of God. It is a bargain at any price. Whether you encounter it when not looking or after you have been searching a long, long time, the kingdom of God is worth whatever it takes to possess it.

Notice that the field hand acted with joy, not reluctantly. This was not a telephone solicitation during dinner. He did not have to be talked into this deal. He was so excited that he could hardly contain himself and couldn't wait to find a buyer for all his other stuff. He really wanted the deed to that property, and he got it. Whenever the merchant found that one special pearl, he let go of everything. He was called crazy by his friends and business associates, so he let go of them also and gained the one thing that made his life worthwhile. Many people had examined and coveted that pearl before this merchant laid his eyes on it; but unlike the merchant, they were content to spend the rest of their lives talking about this wonderful pearl they had seen, how large it was, how perfectly shaped it was, what a beautiful, soft luster it had.

Many people are doing just that today—talking about what a wonderful religion Christ offers—how simple and practical it is, how joyful and fulfilling it is, how peaceful and satisfying it is—but they never claim it as their own, never possess it, never give their all to have it. The emphasis in these two parables is on a sound sense of value, the ability to recognize something of worth, and the determination necessary to possess it. Jesus is stating that God's kingdom of peace and love and hope and joy is the greatest treasure in the world and worth any price to possess.

There is a story in the Gospels about a young man who found this greatest of bargains, this pearl of great price, this treasure hidden in the earth, but unlike the merchant and the field hand, he was not willing to make the necessary investment to claim it. He was a rich young ruler who came to Jesus in search of his greater good: eternal life.

Jesus was willing to offer him what he wanted and said, "Go sell all you have, and come follow me."

When the young man heard the price, he thought, *Too expensive. I can't do it.*

With the field hand and the merchant there was happiness and joy, but with the rich young ruler there was sadness. His countenance fell, and he walked away with a heavy heart from the greatest bargain in the world. He had the means to possess eternal life. He had the means to outbid the field hand and the merchant for the property and the pearl, but he valued the things of this world more than the things of heaven. So he walked away with his fingers closed tightly around his possessions and left the treasure to all the field hands and pearl merchants. Dante described his action as he walked away as "the greatest refusal." I have often wondered what became of that young man.

Jesus came into Galilee preaching the gospel of the kingdom of God and saying, "The time is at hand. The kingdom of God is within your reach. Repent, and believe the good news!"

The price of the kingdom is to part with everything that prevents God's rule in your life: your favorite sins, your hardened resentments, your selfish pride, your personal agenda, and anything else you know is not worthy of God's kingdom.

What would you give for a clear conscience? Peace of mind? Harmony in your home? A new start in life? What would you give for heaven and eternal life? Perhaps you are like the filed hand and do not expect to find anything of value as you go through life, attend church, pray, and read your Bible. But unexpectedly, the spade and the stone have been turned, and something bright and beautiful is revealed. What are you going to do? Or maybe you are like the pearl merchant and have been looking for a long while for something worthy of your total commitment. Well, here it is. It is called the kingdom of God. What are you going to do?

It would be a disservice not to provide an opportunity for

someone to say yes to this greatest of bargains. In the closet of your mind, silently pray this prayer:

> Blessed Jesus, thank You for this opportunity.
> I repent of my sins and ask You into my life.
> I give up everything to own this treasure You offer.
> I give You the payment of my fully devoted life.
> Take my life from this day forward, and make it your own. Amen

EIGHT

THE GREATEST DECISION

Read Matthew 27:15–23.

When we are born and begin to grow as infants there is always someone who decides things for us—what we eat, what we wear, where we live, what time we go to bed, where we go to church, and so on. As we grow older, we learn to make our own decisions. Little by little, and with much pain suffered by our parents (and ourselves), we become independent and finally leave home to make our own way in the world. At first our decisions are simple ones, but eventually they become more complicated, until at last we begin to make decisions that have far-reaching consequences for our own lives and the lives of those around us. Some of these decisions might include: What school should I attend after high school—college or trade school? What career should I invest my life in? Who is the person I will marry?

Where will we live and raise our family? Should I change jobs, sell the house, uproot my family, and move to some other part of the country? How far in debt do I dare to go? These are all important decisions with consequences.

There comes a time when we are called upon to make the greatest of all decisions. This time may come early in childhood, later in the teen years, or later still in the adult years. The decision may be encountered on a printed page, on the television or radio, through a friend, or in a worship service at church.

This decision is in response to the question asked in Matthew 27 by Pilate to the crowd gathered before him: "What am I going to do about Jesus Christ?"

That was the horn of a dilemma upon which Pilate found himself. He was the judge and found his role most uncomfortable. He had to decide the fate of a man who he believed in his heart was innocent. At the same time, he was aware of the ugly mood of the crowd in the courtyard below his balcony. The burden of his conscience was compounded by uneasiness over the identity of this Jesus. From her dreams his wife knew Him to be a just man. From Jesus's own lips he'd heard that He claimed to be king of the Jews. By Jesus's reputation he knew of His claim to be the Son of God.

It was not an enviable position for Pilate. He was doomed if he did, doomed if he didn't. Sly as a fox and slippery as an eel, he sidestepped his responsibility and put it on the crowd.

Let them decide, he thought. *Let it be their decision and not mine.* Who do you want?" Pilate asked. "Jesus or Barabbas?"

They answered, "Barabbas!"

Wrong answer, he thought.

"What then shall I do with Jesus?" he asked.

"Crucify Him!" they answered.

Wrong answer again, he thought.

He then washed his hands of the whole affair, as if a conscience so smitten and stained could be pacified so easily.

Just as Pilate found Jesus on his hands, we too have Jesus on ours.

Pilate's question becomes our question: *What shall I do with Jesus, the Christ?*

> There are several possible answers to the question. We may try to *put Jesus away.* This is what the chief priests, the scribes, the Pharisees, the Sanhedrin, and the mob tried to do, along with Pilate. So they whipped Him at the post, nailed Him to a cross, and sealed Him in a tomb. But Jesus escaped their attempts to put Him away. After three days He rose from the dead and was on their hands again, and with Him came the question again—"What am I to do with this Jesus who refuses to be put away?"

Today there are still those people who try to put Jesus away—put Him out of their society, put Him out of their schools, put Him out of their lives, put Him out of their government, put Him out of their world. But they cannot. Jesus is still on their hands. He cannot be put away.

We may try to *put Jesus off*. That has been a popular response from the beginning. Paul preached Christ to Governor Felix, but Felix told Paul, "Go away for now; when I have a convenient time I will call for you" (Acts 24:25 NKJV).

Felix was deciding not to decide now. That is a dangerous decision. We have no record that Felix ever summoned Paul again to decide for Christ. Many come within the sound of the Gospel and put off their decision for Christ. Week after week they delay, and the longer they delay the easier it is to keep putting Jesus off.

Paul may have been remembering Felix's fatal delay when he wrote to the Corinthians, "Behold, now is the acceptable time; behold, now is the day of salvation" (2 Corinthians 6:2 NKJV).

Another thing we do is *put Jesus aside*. In Luke 18:18–23 a person we call the rich young ruler came running to Jesus with a question burning in his heart. The answer to the question was the only thing he did not possess, and not possessing it made his life miserable.

Casting aside social graces, he threw himself in Jesus's path and asked, "What must I do to inherit eternal life?"

When Jesus was satisfied the man had met all other criteria for what he was seeking He said, "One thing you are missing; Go and sell what you have, give it to the poor, and then come and follow me."

His countenance fell. Wrong answer! He came for an answer and discovered instead a decision. With head hung low, he put Jesus aside and went on his way.

People do that today. We want a painless discipleship. We want to travel through life on shock absorbers. We want to join with those who accept His matchless teachings, but we don't want to sell out to Him. We wish to serve in an advisory capacity. We don't want to preach the Gospel! We don't want to be a missionary! We don't want to be a leader in the church! We don't want to use our gifts in God's work! We don't want to give up *anything*, much less everything! So we put Jesus aside. But it happens with us, as I'm confident it happened with the rich young ruler, that the question follows us wherever we go: What am I going to do with this Jesus who shadows my journey through life and will not be put aside?

One morning in Galilee, lazy waves were lapping the shore of the sea as if yawning at the rising sun. The day was dawning cool and fresh in the Promised Land. Four fishermen were washing their nets and preparing them for their next fishing excursion. They were minding their own business as Jesus strolled down the bank to the edge of the water. He asked them how the catch had gone. He looked over their haul and mentioned something about the price of fish in the market that day. It was small talk.

Then with gentle, piercing eyes he looked at them and said, "Come after me, and I will make you become fishers of men" (Mark 1:17 NKJV).

Pilate's question immediately confronted them in Jesus's invitation. On a moment's notice they had to decide: *What are we going to do with Jesus of Nazareth?* He was right there before them. They could not put Him away or put Him off or put

Him aside. It was the greatest decision of their lives, and it would not wait.

Mark said, "And immediately they left their nets and followed him" (Mark 1:18 NKJV).

We are all making decisions every day concerning Jesus Christ and what to do with Him in our lives. Many centuries ago, the prophet Joel looked upon his world and made this observation, "Multitudes, multitudes in the valley of decision!" (Joel 3:14 NKJV).

All of us have our decision-making valleys. I have mentioned three responses to the question of what to do with Jesus: Put him *away*, put Him *off*, and put Him *aside*. But there is another response. It is the one the disciples made that day beside the sea and the one Paul encouraged for the Christians in Rome. "But put on the Lord Jesus Christ" (Romans 13:14 NKJV).

Don't put Him away or off or aside. Put Him on. Let His word be so much a part of your life that His mind will be in you and His Spirit will be in you. His love will guide you, and His will becomes your will. In such ways do you put on the Lord Jesus. It has been rightly said that great destinies swing on small hinges. Our destinies swing on the small hinge of yes or no to Jesus.

Felix wanted to put his decision off, preferring indecision. I remember going to the beach as a kid with my parents and entering the water exactly in front of the car. Half an hour later I had moved, without realizing it, some twenty yards down the beach. It seemed to me that everything else had moved, for I knew I had not. The waves and the undertow were gently nudging me, inch by inch, farther away from where I wanted to be. In my distraction with the fun I was having, I had made no conscience decision about where I would be. The waves and the undertow moved me along, making the decision for me. If I wanted to remain where my parents were, I had to decide against the forces that were moving me somewhere else. Sometimes we may imagine that no harm comes from our indecision, while in fact the gentle nudging and the undertow of popular opinions, interests, or inclinations, are bearing us away with them, making our decisions for us.

A man is on trial today. His name is Jesus. He is the Son of God, the Savior of the world. Pilate's question is being asked: *What am I to do with Jesus, who is called the Christ?*

You are the judge. You do not wish to be, but like Pilate, there is no one else to decide. You must weigh the evidence and make the decision. What are you going to do with Jesus of Nazareth today?

NINE

THE GREATEST DISASTER

Read Matthew 7:24–29.

I t is important that we recognize the context of this particular parable. It is given as the conclusion to the Sermon on the Mount, which began in chapter 5, verse 1. Literary critics have acclaimed the Sermon on the Mount as the greatest teaching ever addressed to the human family. Many today readily agree that this collection of the teachings of Jesus is the truest, the noblest, and the best guide we have for living. But Jesus is not going to let us be content in our admiration of His words. He is not going to let us pass them off with high-sounding praise or place them in a category with other great teachings. Admiration or flattery is not the response Jesus is looking for.

His was an authoritative word, and He tells us quite plainly, "Your response to my teachings will either make you or break you as you go through life. What you do about what you hear from me will determine the eventual success or failure of your life. Your eternal destiny hangs on the thread of your response to the words I have spoken."

In light of this there is not a more important collection of writing in the world than that found in the Gospel of Jesus Christ. Jesus tells us there are two responses to His teachings. He says, in effect, "I will show you what these responses may be compared to. Listen well because what you are about to hear is more important to you than wealth or fame or power. Everyone who hears these words of mine and does not obey them will be like a foolish man who built his house upon the sand."

People hear the words of Jesus in Sunday school or church small groups or family devotions. Perhaps they read the Bible from cover to cover or studied the Bible well enough to have memorized a hundred or more passages of scripture. Jesus says that is not enough.

Some people live thinking that when they arrive at the pearly gates Saint Peter will say, "Quote me some scripture." And if they come up with Psalm 23, John 3:16, or Romans 12:1, he will then say, "Good enough, come on in."

That is not the way it will be. Jesus says God is going to thump our foundations to test what they are made of.

What exactly makes for a foundation of sand? The Sermon on the Mount teaches us that a sandy foundation is a life based upon sensual pleasures (5:27–30), trusting one's possessions for security (6:19), pride (6:1–18), rejection of the straight and narrow way (7:13, 14)—in other words, throwing off moral restraint and spiritual discipline, expecting to enter through heaven's gate along the broadway of the world.

To these Jesus says, "Don't you understand that you cannot walk the way of the world and the way of my kingdom at the same time? Don't you understand that two roads so different will lead to two different destinations?"

Having a superficial religion makes for a sandy foundation. Chapter 5, verse 20 says, "Unless your righteousness exceeds the righteousness of the scribes and Pharisees, you will never enter the kingdom of God."

Then follows a set of six teachings in which Jesus illustrates that superficial religion is inadequate in our quests for God's kingdom. These illustrations may be called the "But I say Unto Yous" of Jesus. They deal with matters of our behavior.

"You have heard it said you shall not murder, you shall not commit adultery, divorce is okay, you shall not swear, eye for eye, tooth for tooth, love only those who love you. That is shallow and superficial religion. If you think you are going to make it to heaven by just getting by, forget it. You're building on sand," says Jesus, "and God is going to thump your foundation."

What is the final consequence of those who have heard but do not obey the teachings of Jesus? "And the rain descended, the floods came, and the wind blew and beat on that house, and it fell" (Matthew 7:27 NKJV).

It fell! The house crumbled, and the life caved in. Within the sound of saving grace, it was devastated by disobedience, crushed under the weight of rejection. Simply to say that the house fell does not suffice to convey the measure of the disaster that overwhelmed that house.

Jesus added this commentary: "And great was its fall."

On Thursday, May 8, 1902, on an island in the West Indies, the volcano Mount Pelée exploded into a solid wall of flame that rolled over the city of Saint-Pierre. Almost instantly a searing wave of heat killed all but two of the thirty thousand inhabitants. Within seconds Saint-Pierre, once known as the Paris of the West Indies, reappeared, stripped of every recognizable landmark as though it were an ancient ruin recently excavated. That was a major disaster.

Measured by the destruction of property and the loss of life, our own history has known its share of disasters: earthquakes, tornados, hurricanes, drought. But far greater than these is the disaster Jesus describes as the fall of one eternal soul. "And great was the fall of it." The loss was beyond measure. The disaster had no equal.

Jesus asked, "For what will it profit a man if he gains the whole world, and loses his own soul?" (Mark 8:36 NKJV).

The loss of a soul is by far the greatest of all disasters. Cities can be rebuilt; fields can be replanted; other ships, planes, trains, and automobiles can be built; but a lost soul is irreplaceable. It is a loss beyond recovery. There are no copies, no duplicates. There's only one you. Is it any wonder, then, that Jesus, with a sigh of sadness, added the words: *and great was the fall of it?*

Hear the words of our Lord further. "Everyone who hears these words of mine and obeys them will be like a wise man who built his house upon the rock" (Matthew 7:24).

What makes for a foundation of rock? Again, we look to the Sermon on the Mount.

- Hungering and thirsting after righteousness (Matthew 5:5)
- Purity of heart (Matthew 5:8)
- Being done with superficial religion (Matthew 5:20–48)
- Singleness of devotion to the Lord, Jesus Christ (Matthew 6:24)
- Giving priority to God's kingdom of righteousness (Matthew 6:33)
- Adopting the discipline of the straight and narrow way (Matthew 7:13)

"Obey my teachings," says Jesus, "and you will be equipped to endure the storms of life."

What happens to a house built upon the rock? The same things that happen to a sand-based house. The rains fell, the floods came, the wind blew against that house, but … but … it did not fall, because it was founded upon the rock.

In Matthew 24:35 (NKJV), Jesus said, "Heaven and earth shall pass away, but My words will by no means pass away."

Is it any wonder then, that the teachings of Jesus are foundations of stone—eternal, fixed forever, more enduring than Gibraltar or Everest? Whoever builds their lives on His teachings will endure forever. Jesus tells us that in all of life there is the prospect of rescue or ruin, deliverance or disaster. It all depends on how we respond to His teachings.

TEN

THE GREATEST SACRIFICE

Read John 19:1–18.

The sacrificial rituals advocated in the Old Testament and practiced by ancient Jews are quite alien to us. We do not understand why anything should die simply because we do something wrong. However, since the exodus from Eden, a sentence has been passed that "the soul that sins will surely die." There is a penalty for transgressing the holiness of God.

Since we were created in God's image, our sins do indeed transgress His holiness. We are not particularly aware of being created in God's image; therefore, we do not acknowledge the acute seriousness of our sins whenever we commit them. The more insensitive we become to sinning, the less we are able to comprehend the holiness of God and the purpose of the Old

Testament sacrifices. A sacrifice was an atonement for sins committed.

The Hebrew word *atonement* means "to cover" or "to secure from guilt." The word conveys the idea of turning away the wrath of God and covering the sins of the guilty party (Vines Word Studies). Because of the seriousness of sin, there was only one thing of great enough value to satisfy the penalty for sin. That one thing was blood. The writer of Hebrews observed that "without the shedding of blood there is no forgiveness" (Hebrews 9:22 NIV).

Why blood? The book of Leviticus explains why: "For the life of the creature is in the blood, and I have given it to you to make atonement for yourselves on the altar; it is the blood that makes atonement for one's life" (Leviticus 17:11 NIV). Life is the most precious commodity in all of creation. Because blood is the vehicle of life and sustains the life of every living thing, its value is great enough to cover our transgressions and satisfy the penalty for our violations against a holy God.

The Jews celebrated their festivals of sacrifice with both joy and humility. Humility because they were guilty before God. Joy because their sins were covered and they had been given a clean start in life. Perhaps if we had a higher view of the holiness of God, we could better understand and appreciate the rituals of sacrifice in the Old Testament.

There were some great sacrifices offered in the history of Israel. In 2 Chronicles 29, Hezekiah becomes king in Israel. His father, Ahaz, had been unfaithful to the Lord. During Ahaz's sixteen-year reign he sacrificed his children in the fire as an offering to foreign gods; he desecrated the Temple, using its treasures to bribe the king of Assyria to protect him; he took away the furnishings of the Temple, snuffed out the holy lamps, and shut the doors of the Lord's house.

"For the Lord brought Judah low because of king Ahaz king of Israel, for he had encouraged moral decline in Judah and had been continually unfaithful to the Lord" (2 Chronicles 28:19 NKJV).

Following Ahaz, Hezekiah campaigned to restore the Temple to its holy purpose. He reopened its doors, returned its furnishings, and relit the holy lamps. After all of this, they had a great celebration of repentance. "Also the burnt offerings were in abundance, with the fat of the peace offerings and with the drink offerings for every burnt offering. So the service of the house of the Lord was set in order" (2 Chronicles 29:35 NKJV).

After this they decided to celebrate Passover in May rather than the normal time in April. The Passover had not been observed for a long time, so a proclamation was sent out. At the appointed time the celebration began and continued for eight days. They offered many sacrifices to God and confessed their sins. Then the people were filled with deep joy. Jerusalem had not seen a celebration like that one since the days of Solomon.

When Hezekiah died his son, Manasseh, reigned for fifty-five years. He did evil in the sight of the Lord—even more than had his grandfather Ahaz. After him his son, Amon, reigned for two short years, continuing the evil practices of his father. After fifty-seven years of debauchery Josiah the Righteous, great grandson of Hezekiah, grandson of wicked Manasseh, son of evil Amon, ascended to the throne. Josiah did what was right in the eyes of the Lord. He repaired the Temple and restored its worship, He renewed the covenant made through Abraham and Moses, and he reinstituted the Passover observance.

"There had been no Passover kept in Israel like that since the days of Samuel the prophet; and none of the kings of Israel had kept such a Passover as Josiah kept ... In the eighteenth year of the reign of Josiah this Passover was kept" (2 Chronicles 35:18, 19 NKJV).

These were indeed great celebrations of repentance and renewal with great sacrifices attending them, but there was never an end of them. The sacrifices had to be repeated because the sins of the people kept reoccurring over and over again. Sacrifices removed the guilt of the sinners, but they had no power to change the hearts of the sinners. Sacrifices could cover the sins of the people, but they could not remove the stain of their sins. The applied blood of the sacrifice could make the outside of the sinner ceremonially clean, but it could not cleanse the conscience or purge the heart of the desire for sin. To accomplish something of the magnitude necessary to cleanse and change the hearts of humankind and deal with the cause rather than the symptoms of sin would require a sacrifice of much greater value than the blood of bulls, lambs, and goats. Therefore, God made provision for a greater sacrifice. It came about as described in John 19:1–18.

On Palm Sunday, Jesus, God's perfect sacrifice, entered Jerusalem with shouts of, "Blessed is He who comes in the name of the Lord."

But they did not understand.

On Thursday of that week Jesus celebrated the Passover meal with His apostles. He instituted the Lord's Supper, saying the bread was His body and the wine was His blood. He commanded this ritual as a perpetual remembrance of His death until He came again.

But they did not understand.

Later that night, in the garden of Gethsemane, He was arrested and tried for treason against the Roman empire and sedition against the Jewish state. It was the soldier's prerogative to make sport of condemned criminals. The Roman guards mocked Jesus with a crown of thorns and a purple robe. They scourged Him with a whip and slapped and spat upon Him. Throughout the night He suffered indignities, never saying a mumbling word.

Friday morning the verdict was sealed. He was taken from His cell, tried before Pilate and the people, and condemned to die by crucifixion. He was placed in procession with two others and marched outside the city walls. A cross was laid on His back. With the help of one named Simon, He carried the instrument of His torture to the place of His death. He carried His own altar to the place of His sacrifice. They call the route of His death procession the *Via Dolorosa*.

> La Via Dolorosa, the way of pain for Him.
> Stone pavement rushes up to meet His leaden limbs
> While crowds of cross-less, Christ-less faces

Sway before His clouded eyes,
The cross hangs heavy on His bleeding back
And flings His knees in anguish to the ground.
He bows His head beneath the load and cries.
He reels, and falls, and rises, and again
He hoists the wooden cross above His head
And sets His face to Calvary.
La Via Dolorosa … the way of gain for me.
(Loretta J. Jenkins)

Because of its shape, they called the place of His execution Golgotha, "skull hill." It was there they laid the cross on the ground and laid Him on the cross. Two soldiers held His arms as another drove spikes through His wrists into the wood. They drew up His knees just short of a thirty-degree angle and nailed His feet to the upright beam. Then they lifted the cross upright. The weight of His body now hung upon the nails.

They positioned the base of the cross near a four-foot-deep hole that had been dug to plant it in. They let the cross slide into the hole with a jolt. When it hit bottom, His body tore at the nails. The pain sent His nervous system into shock for a few minutes. Then the full measure of His tortures began. About six hours later death had mercy on Him, and He died.

This was no accident of fate that happened to Jesus that day. It was no misfortune of circumstances that carried Him to that hour. A Scottish professor walked back and forth on the platform as he discoursed with his students on the crucifixion.

"D'ye know," he asked. "D'ye know what it was—dyin'

on a cross—forsaken by His Father? D'ye know what it was? What? What? It was damnation, I tell ya—and damnation taken lovingly" (Hastings, 1 Corinthians, pg. 424).

We cannot be expected to understand the crucifixion; it is the wisdom and power of God. The writer of Hebrews explained the sacrifice of Jesus in chapters nine and ten. He declared that Christ appeared once for all at the end of the age to do away with sin by sacrificing Himself.

Christ was sacrificed to take away the sins of the world. This was by far a greater sacrifice, superior to the former ones, because it goes to the heart of mankind and deals with the root cause of sin and not just its symptoms. This is what is meant in Jeremiah 31:31–33 (NKJV), "Behold, the days are coming," says the Lord, "when I will make a new covenant with the house of Israel and with the house of Judah … I will put My law in their minds and write it on their hearts."

The blood of Jesus shed on the cross has become the guarantee of a better covenant. It makes atonement, not by covering, but by cleansing. It deflects the wrath of God through this dispensation of grace. When the mercy gates are lifted and the flood of God's wrath overwhelms the sinners because of the hardness and wickedness of their hearts, the blood of Christ upon the doorpost of the heart will cause God's wrath to pass over those who have claimed Christ as their Redeemer. Peace has been made with God through the blood of Christ's greater sacrifice on an old rugged cross. (See Colossians 1:20.)

ELEVEN

THE GREATEST VICTORY

Read Matthew 28:1–7.

D eath does strange things to our psyche. Death goes bump in the night. It is like the noise in the dark when children tell ghost stories around a campfire. No one wants to admit they are afraid, so they laugh up some courage. Where we go when we die is a subject of great concern to us.

An epitaph in an English churchyard read:

> Remember man that passeth by,
> As you are now so once was I;
> And as I am you soon must be,
> Prepare yourself to follow me.

Under this someone had written:
> To follow you I'm not content,
> Until I know which way you went.

Even though death may have the final say, we at least wish to have the last laugh. There are some things in life too serious for anything but laughter.

We love life dearly, but there are two things that destroy life: sin and death. These are the twin tragedies visited upon the human experience from that paradise called Eden. In the Old Testament, sin had its remedies in sacrifices; but there was no remedy for death. No matter how good a person was, they always died. Both the righteous and the unrighteous became the banquet for decay. From the end of Eden, death has held humankind in a vice-like grip of despair.

But God had a plan. He promised through the prophet Hosea, "I will ransom them from the power of the grave; I will redeem them from death" (Hosea 13:14 NKJV).

The greatness of the Gospel is that death's grip of despair has been broken. It began on the cross of Christ and ended in His empty tomb. In the hour of His agony Jesus could have called seventy-two thousand angels to destroy the world and set Him free, but He did not call them (Matthew 26:53). Jesus was doing battle as He died. It was a great battle against the two destroyers of life: sin and death. He must not avoid the cross and He must not call the angels. His eye was fixed, and His heart was set on a great victory. There can be no great victories where there are no great battles.

When Jesus died it appeared to the world He had failed. "Cursed is everyone who hangs upon a tree," was the verdict of sacred writings. To be crucified meant your name would be blotted from the family record and your memory erased from the pages of history.

When Jesus died His heart stopped beating, His body became cold and clay-like. His eyes glazed over, and His limbs became stiff. His body was taken from the cross, wrapped in cloth, and laid on the cold slab of a tomb. A massive stone was rolled against the opening of the tomb, barring light, insuring darkness. Roman guards were posted. Everyone went home. and the world went back to the way it was before He came. All that was left were a few glorious memories, which in time would fade and fall, just as He had done. When Jesus died, it appeared to all the world that He had failed. He had lost the battle and the cause He had championed.

In our sphere of time and history, we are limited to seeing only a fraction of reality. There is a realm beyond our sight. What could not be observed was that when Jesus died it sent a shudder throughout the domain of death. A wild-eyed Satan grabbed hold of the pillars of his kingdom as its foundations quaked and his empire crumbled down around him. The enemy of all that is fair and lovely had shaken his fist in the face of God, had boasted in his plan to ruin the handiwork of the Creator, and had recruited an army of angelic infidels to assault the heart of God by the ruin of all that God loves.

This bold adversary ranted and raged on Golgotha's brow because he dreaded nothing more than the death of the righteous Son of God. He had tried with all his cunning to tempt Jesus to sin and stain the sacrifice of Himself. Having failing in this, he wanted Jesus to keep on living, avoid the crisis of the cross, and waste away with a long life and a harmless death. He had tried everything to undo redemption's plan. But Jesus had fought the enemy all the way, step-by-step resisting his unholy suggestions and spurning his pitiful promises.

In Gethsemane Jesus overcame the final assault. All the demons that gnawed at His nerves were sent scurrying back to their hellish holes when He said to His Father, "Nevertheless, not my will but thine be done."

The devil let out a scream of frustration.

Jesus had gone with the soldiers and stood before Pilate. He had taken His beatings and carried His cross. His eye had been fixed and His heart set on a great victory, and there can be no great victories where there are no great battles.

At Jesus's tomb, in the early morning hours of the first day of the week, the soldiers guarding the tomb heard a bump in the night and felt the ground tremble beneath their boots. They watched in wide-eyed wonder as the great stone against the entrance of the tomb rolled backward and up the incline, seemingly of its own accord. An unearthly light glowed behind the stone until it flooded the garden with glory. Their startled eyes witnessed Jesus, heart pumping, eyes bright, flesh warm, and limbs limber, stepping from the tomb.

"Good morning, boys!" He said.

The soldiers fainted.

Jesus, the Son of God, had just accomplished the greatest victory over a formidable enemy the world has ever known. The world has never been the same since that memorable morning. After Resurrection morning, death was no longer the dreaded menace it had once been.

Jesus had gone through the grave and come back. He'd smiled and said, "Don't be afraid. I have removed the sting from this enemy."

After this, the New Testament writers said things like "Not even death can separate us from the love of God," "Death has been swallowed up in victory," and "Christ has abolished death."

As if to thumb his nose at death, Paul wrote, "Ha! O Death, where is your sting now? Mr. Grave, where is your victory?"

The miracle of that resurrection morning is not only that we will live forever when we die, but also that we can live triumphantly before we die. We can live the resurrected life today.

We can be done with sin and shame. We can let go of doubts and worries. We can release our fears and suspicions. We can repent of our sins and step out of the shadows of uncertainty and into the light of a life surrendered to Jesus Christ.

Bishop Fulton J. Sheen once said, "Unrepented lives are like a man who spent his entire life in prison not knowing the door was unlocked ... because he never tried it."

The Bible says that Jesus shared in our humanity so that by His death He might be victorious over the power of death and set free all those who were held in slavery all their lives by their fear of death (Hebrews 2:15). Jesus unlocked the door of our prison.

It was not just a battle Jesus won when He stepped out of that tomb. He had won the war, and seventy-two thousand angels sang a hymn of Resurrection!

Printed in the United States
by Baker & Taylor Publisher Services